DR. ABBOTT FORD

We are to treat our wives better

First and foremost, I would like to thank God for giving me this testimony to help others

And the Lord God said, It is not good that the man should be alone; I will make him an help meet for him.

Genesis 2:18-23 (KJV)

Contents

Acknowledgement

Thank you for purchasing this book. As an old man, I have always wanted to write a book that could influence positivity for the greater good of humanity. I've felt the need to write about a topic that I've personally experienced over the years, in the hopes that it might help someone in need. I truly wish there had been a book like this during my younger days—perhaps it could have saved me some time and helped me be a better husband to my wife.

I hope this book serves its purpose by helping someone who is suffering from marriage problems. In my younger days, there weren't many books discussing topics like this, so I feel fortunate to be able to contribute to the library of resources that might help someone now and for many years to come.

I thank my wife for not giving up on me—I will always love you. And to my children, I love you and am so proud of everything you have become.
    Also a special thanks to

Olivia Johnson
Ethan Parker Ava Smith Liam Wilson
Emma Thompson Noah Anderson
Sophia Brown Mason Davis
Isabella Clark Lucas Miller
Mia Taylor Amelia Harris
Elijah Martin Charlotte Robinson James White.   Harper
Lewis
Benjamin Walker Grace Hall
Henry Young Evelyn King
Alexander Wright Scarlett Scott
William Green Abigail Adams
Jackson Baker Ella Perez
Michael Mitchell Lily Carter
Daniel Roberts
Aria Campbell Aiden Evans
Chloe Hill Matthew Rivera
Emily Collins Joseph Ramirez
Madison Sanchez Samuel Stewart
Avery Cook David Barnes
Scarlett Hughes Andrew Ross
Zoey Morgan Nathan Powell
Natalie Sanders Caleb Patterson
Nora Gray Joshua Butler
Lillian Jenkins Christopher Long
Audrey Kelly Ryan Ward
Hannah Brooks Isaiah Foster
Penelope Richardson John Perry
Victoria Russell Thomas Watson
Lucy James Luke Coleman
Zoe Bryant Leo Griffin

Riley Henderson Isaac Phillips
Stella Reed Sebastian Torres
Paisley Hayes Owen Ramirez
Aurora Turner Gabriel Murphy
Ellie Sanders Julian Brooks
Leah Cook Levi Reed Camila Howard
Dylan Simmons

Preface

This book is a heartfelt exploration of the profound impact of marriage when viewed through a Christian lens. Authored by Dr. Abbott Ford, a dedicated physician and loving family man, the text offers a deeply personal perspective on the sacred bond of marriage. Abbott draws from his own experiences, reflecting on his journey from a flawed understanding of marital roles to a deeper, more enlightened appreciation of love and commitment.

In these pages, Abbott shares candidly about his early misconceptions of marriage, including his misguided beliefs about control and servitude. Through introspection and spiritual growth, he reveals how embracing a genuine Christian approach—marked by unconditional love, respect, and service—transformed his relationship with his wife and strengthened their family dynamic.

Abbott's reflections are enriched by his professional background and his faith, providing a unique vantage point on how to navigate the complexities of marriage while staying true to one's spiritual values. This book is not only a testament to the personal growth Abbott has undergone but also a guide for others seeking to build a marriage that reflects divine principles and endures through life's trials and triumphs.

My wife put aside her desire to start her own business. She always wanted to be a chef and own a restaurant—anything to do with cooking, she was fine with it. However, as my career elevated to the point where I wasn't able to keep my end of the bargain from the beginning of our marriage, her dreams were put on hold. I had already spent a lot of time dedicating myself to my education to become a doctor. She supported me during my years of studying. I told her that after eight years, I would be able to help support her dreams. But unfortunately, we had to change that agreement because we figured it would be more suitable for our children to be homeschooled. As a result, she quit her job and stayed home to homeschool the kids.

She did it all—the cooking, the cleaning, washing clothes, folding clothes, and schooling the kids on their lessons. Every time she brought up the possibility of starting a new career and putting the kids in private school, I would get upset. It was just easier and safer for us to keep homeschooling the kids until we moved. We had enough income to take care of the family, and she didn't need to work. I was bringing in all the money; all she had to do was cook, clean, and school the kids. That's all. I didn't understand why it was such a big deal. I figured that as long as I was providing, she could do her part at least.

I got tired of hearing excuses, and every time I turned around, it was another subject about spending money. If it wasn't about putting the kids in private school and her going back to work, it was about spending large amounts of money on unnecessary things. She would buy all these cooking books; she had a chef's library with shelves filled with DIY cooking books. It made me sick. I would come home, and she'd be reading another book on cooking. I felt it would be a waste of time if she wasn't cooking the things she was reading about.

One afternoon, my wife, Sara, received a call that filled her with both excitement and a tinge of anxiety. Her close group of girlfriends from college, women she hadn't seen in over five years, were coming into town. They had all gone their separate ways after graduation, each carving out her own path in life, and the opportunity to reconnect after so long was both thrilling and daunting.

Sara eagerly invited them to our home, feeling a wave of nostalgia wash over her as she thought of the memories they had shared during their college days. These were the women who had seen her through some of the most transformative years of her life—years filled with late-night study sessions, spontaneous road trips, and deep conversations about their dreams for the future.

When the day arrived, Sara prepared the house with care, making sure everything was perfect. She wanted her friends to feel at home, to see that despite the years that had passed, their bond was still strong. However, there was a lingering worry in the back of her mind, one that she tried to push aside as she busied herself with last-minute preparations.

When her friends arrived, the house was filled with laughter and chatter, the sound of old friends catching up as though no time had passed at all. They embraced each other warmly, reminiscing about their college days, sharing updates on their lives, and marveling at how much had changed.

But as the conversation continued, Sara's friends began to ask questions—questions about her life, her marriage, and how things had turned out for her since they last saw each other. One of her friends, Emily, who had always been the most outspoken of the group, couldn't help but comment on how glamorous Sara's life must be, being married to a doctor.

"You must have everything you want," Emily said with a smile, her tone laced with a mix of envy and admiration. "Your husband is a doctor! I know you must be living the good life— no worries, no struggles. I wish I could say the same about my life. My husband and I have to work double time just to make ends meet."

The other women nodded in agreement, each of them sharing their own stories of the challenges they faced in their careers and marriages. Amanda, who had become a lawyer, spoke about the long hours she put in at her firm, often feeling like she was sacrificing her personal life for her career. Nicole, who had pursued a career in education, talked about the strain of balancing her work as a high school teacher with her responsibilities as a mother of three. Ruth , who had started her own business, shared the constant stress of managing a small company and the pressure to keep it afloat. And then there was Lisa, who had become a nurse, expressing the emotional toll her job had taken on her, especially during difficult times.

As each woman shared her story, Sara listened intently, nodding in understanding and offering words of encouragement. But when it came time for her to speak about her own life, she hesitated. She wasn't as enthusiastic as her friends might have expected, and she found herself struggling to explain how her life had turned out.

Yes, she was married to a doctor, and from the outside, her life might have seemed perfect—financially secure, comfortable, and without the same struggles her friends were facing. But the reality was far more complex, and it wasn't something she could easily put into words.

Sara had always been the type to keep her struggles to herself. She didn't want to burden others with her problems, especially not her friends who were already dealing with so much in their own lives. So, instead of delving into the truth of her situation, she simply laughed it off, deflecting their questions with light-hearted comments and changing the subject whenever the conversation veered too close to her own challenges.

The truth was, Sara's life was not as glamorous as her friends imagined. While they talked about their careers and the pride they took in their work, Sara thought about how different her path had been. She had always dreamed of becoming a chef, of owning her own restaurant and sharing her passion for cooking with the world. But those dreams had been put on hold when we decided to homeschool our children.

It wasn't that Sara resented her role as a wife and mother—she loved our children deeply, and she took great pride in the job she had done raising them. But there were times when she couldn't help but feel a pang of longing for the life she had once envisioned for herself. The life where she was more than just a wife and a mother, where she was also a successful chef, creating culinary masterpieces and making a name for herself in the world of food.

But that wasn't the life she had. Instead, she found herself in a home filled with cookbooks she rarely had the time to use, surrounded by the tools of a trade she hadn't been able to fully pursue. And while she loved the life we had built together, she couldn't deny that there were times when she felt like something was missing—like a part of her had been left behind in the pursuit of my career and the raising of our children.

So, as her friends talked about their careers and the pride they felt in their work, Sara kept her thoughts to herself. She smiled and nodded, laughed and joked, but she didn't share the full story of her life. She didn't tell them about the sacrifices she had made, or the dreams she had put on hold. She didn't tell them about the loneliness she sometimes felt, or the frustration of feeling like her life had been reduced to a series of roles—

wife, mother, homemaker—without the fulfillment of her own ambitions.

Instead, she listened to her friends' stories, offering support and encouragement, but keeping her own struggles hidden beneath the surface. After all, she didn't want to spoil the reunion with tales of unfulfilled dreams or the complexities of her marriage. She wanted her friends to leave feeling uplifted and happy, not burdened by the weight of her own experiences.

As the day came to a close and her friends prepared to leave, Sara felt a mixture of emotions. She was grateful for the time they had spent together, for the chance to reconnect and reminisce about the past. But she also felt a lingering sadness—a reminder of the life she had once dreamed of and the path she had taken instead.

In the end, Sara knew that she had made the right choices for our family, and she wouldn't trade the life we had built together for anything. But that didn't mean she didn't sometimes wonder about what might have been, about the dreams she had left behind. And as she waved goodbye to her friends, she couldn't help but feel a sense of longing—for the life she had imagined, and for the dreams that still lingered in the back of her mind.

Yet, despite these feelings, Sara remained strong. She had always been resilient, finding joy in the life she had, even when it wasn't exactly what she had envisioned. She was proud of the family she had raised, proud of the love we shared, and proud of the sacrifices she had made to keep our family together. And she knew that, in the end, that was what truly mattered.

As she closed the door behind her friends, Sara took a deep breath and smiled. She knew that life was a journey, filled with twists and turns, and she was ready to continue walking that path—one step at a time, with her family by her side.

The day had been long, and the night seemed even longer as I walked through the door, feeling the weight of the world on my shoulders. Work had been exhausting, filled with pressures and challenges that left me mentally and physically drained. All I wanted to do was retreat to the comfort of my home, unwind, and let the day slip away into a blur of forgetfulness.

As I entered the house, Sara greeted me with a warm smile, eager to share the events of her day. Her friends had left just hours before, and I could see the remnants of excitement still lingering in her eyes. She started to tell me about their visit, recounting the conversations and laughter they had shared. I nodded my head, trying to appear engaged, but the truth was, I wasn't really listening. My mind was still caught up in the whirlwind of work, and all I could think about was how much I just wanted to be left alone.

"Good to hear," I mumbled automatically, my words devoid of any real interest. I was so tired that I could barely keep my eyes open, let alone focus on the details of her day. But I didn't want to seem rude, so I pretended to listen, offering the occasional nod or murmur of agreement. Sara continued to talk, her voice a soft and comforting presence, but it might as well have been background noise to me. I was already half-asleep, my exhaustion winning out over any attempt to stay engaged in the conversation.

And then, in the middle of one of her sentences, I drifted off completely, my head lolling to the side as I began to snore lightly. It didn't take long for Sara to notice, and she gently woke me up, her voice tender and understanding.

"Baby, maybe you should go to sleep," she said softly, concern evident in her tone.

I jolted awake, embarrassed that I had fallen asleep while she was talking. "No, I'm listening," I insisted, trying to shake off the drowsiness. I didn't want to admit that I hadn't really been paying attention, so I forced myself to sit up and focus on what she was saying.

"Okay," Sara replied, though I could tell she wasn't convinced. "I wanted to ask you a question. I was talking it over with my friends, and we're thinking about having a girls' night out. You know, just the girls, like we used to do when we were in college. I'd like to try and hang out with them if it's all right with you, sometime next week."

The request caught me off guard, and I could feel my irritation bubbling up almost immediately. I never liked the idea of Sara going out without me, especially not with her old college friends. It made me uncomfortable, uneasy in a way I couldn't quite explain. And so, instead of considering her request, I lashed out.

"This is not the time to be going out," I snapped. "Our children are in class—who's going to make sure they're doing their schoolwork if you're out gallivanting with your friends?"

Sara's expression faltered, but she tried to explain. "I was thinking of getting a babysitter, or maybe a tutor for that day. It's only going to be one day, and really, only at night. I just want to spend a little time with my friends."

But I wasn't having it. I let my own insecurities and frustrations take over, making her feel guilty for even asking. "No wife needs to be spending the night out without her husband," I said coldly. "Especially not with a bunch of girls from back in the day. What are you even married for if you're going to entertain their presence?"

My words were harsh, and I could see the effect they had on Sara. She broke down, tears welling up in her eyes as she tried to make sense of my reaction. She was frustrated, hurt, and I could tell she felt trapped—trapped by my demands, by my expectations, by the life we had built together.

But then, something shifted in her. She wiped away her tears, took a deep breath, and regained her composure. With a quiet dignity, she looked at me and said, "Never mind, Abbott. If you're not okay with it, then I won't go."

I could see the disappointment in her eyes, the way her shoulders slumped as if she was carrying the weight of my words. It was as if I had snuffed out a small light inside her, leaving her feeling enslaved to my commands. But at the time, I was too angry, too blinded by my own emotions to see the damage I had done. I was just relieved that the issue was settled, that I wouldn't have to worry about her going out and leaving me alone to deal with everything.

"Fine, then it's settled," I said, my voice still laced with irritation. But even as the words left my mouth, I knew something wasn't right. The look on Sara's face haunted me, the way her eyes had lost their spark, the way she seemed so defeated.

That night, as I lay in bed, unable to sleep, I couldn't shake the image of Sara's face from my mind. I had always prided myself on being a good husband, a good father, but in that moment, I realized that I had fallen short. I had let my own pride and stubbornness come between us, and I knew I needed to make things right.

But the shame was overwhelming. I wanted to apologize, to let her know I had been wrong, that I had let my own fears get in the way of her happiness. But I couldn't bring myself to do it. I was too ashamed, too afraid that the damage had already been done, and I didn't know how to fix it.

So, I said nothing. The next morning, I woke up with a heavy heart, knowing I should have apologized, but instead, I let the moment pass. I went on with my day, trying to push the guilt away, but the image of Sara's disappointed face stayed with me, a constant reminder of the words I hadn't said.

The reminder of life

Two weeks later, I get the phone call that shook my world. My grandfather call me in tears. I couldn't believe it my grandfather on my mom's side was so devastated about his wife. They were always arguing about everything the next minute loving each other a real marriage ,despite their rollercoaster of love , they lived to be in their 90s and traveled everywhere together. Then, on that unfortunate day when my grandma passed away, I saw something that changed my perspective entirely about my marriage to Sara and I pray never to have to experience it . I had never seen so much hurt on a man's face. It was then that I realized my grandfather truly will broken-hearted for the rest of his life —she was the love of his life.

They met when she was 15, back when they were in school, and they started dating. And get this—they were virgins all the way up to the day they got married. After grandma passed, my grandpa didn't live much longer. A few months later, he joined her. I express all this to say that when you love somebody, yes, you argue, and you don't always share the same ideas. But when that person is no longer around, how will you maintain? My grandfather died from a broken heart. He truly loved his wife—my grandma. It was a hard year, watching my mom go through all that loss, losing both her parents.

I remember going to their house to clean it out. In my grandparents' bedroom, the pictures, the memories, and the energy of love left in that house—it was enough to make you cry. I remember picking up a picture of my grandparents when they were in their teens. They were so youthful, with so much love in their eyes. My grandfather had told me a lot about their marriage. No matter how hard things got, they stayed together. It was said that when my grandfather was found, he was sitting in a rocking chair with tears in his eyes, holding onto a picture of his wife. A VHS tape was playing on the television—a video of him and my grandma. One video showed them walking on the beach, holding hands, laughing, and enjoying each other's company.

As I reflect on my grandfather's life, I often wonder how he must have felt spending so many years with someone he loved, only to reach a point where he had to face the harsh reality that she was no longer there. They shared a lifetime together, witnessing the world change in ways they could never have imagined—from a time of minimal technology to the rapid advancements that now shape our daily lives. My grandfather used to tell stories about his time in the army, often recounting the storms he faced not only in battle but also in his heart, being separated from my grandmother. The world was so different then, and the challenges they faced were immense. He struggled through that separation for a whole year, not knowing what the future held or if he would ever return to the life he had known.

My grandfather was a young man when he enlisted in the army, driven by a sense of duty to his country and a desire to protect the freedoms that so many before him had fought to preserve. The world was embroiled in conflict, and he felt a deep responsibility to do his part. The decision to leave home was not an easy one, especially knowing that he would be leaving behind his wife, my grandmother. They had only been married for a short time, their love still fresh and full of the promise of a future together. But the war called, and he answered, knowing that his absence would bring uncertainty and fear.

The year he spent away from home was one of the most challenging periods of his life. He was stationed in a distant land, far from the familiar comforts of home. The days were long and grueling, filled with the constant threat of danger and the relentless pressure to stay vigilant. Yet, in the midst of the chaos, his thoughts were never far from my grandmother. He would often write her letters, pouring his heart onto the pages, hoping that his words could somehow bridge the distance between them. He wrote about the conditions he faced—the harsh weather, the scarcity of supplies, the camaraderie among the soldiers, and the fear that gripped him in the quiet moments when the fighting ceased.

The day he returned home was one of the happiest days of their lives. The war had taken its toll on him, both physically and emotionally, but the sight of my grandmother waiting for him at the train station was enough to erase the pain of the past year. They embraced as if they would never let go, the relief of being together again washing over them in waves. The world outside may have been uncertain, but in that moment, all that mattered was that they were together.

Shortly after his return, they began to build the life they had always dreamed of. It wasn't long before my grandmother became pregnant with my mother. The news brought immense joy to their lives, marking the beginning of a new chapter. My mother's birth was a beacon of hope, a sign that life could go on after the war, that love could prevail even in the darkest of times. She was born into a world that was still healing, but the love that surrounded her was unwavering. My grandfather doted on my mother from the moment she was born, cherishing every moment he could spend with her. He had seen the worst that the world had to offer, and it made him appreciate the simple joys of family life even more.

As my mother grew, the bond between my grandparents only strengthened. They had faced the ultimate test of their love and had come out on the other side, more committed to each other than ever before. My grandfather's experiences in the army had changed him, but they had also deepened his appreciation for the life he had built with my grandmother. He never took a single day for granted, always making sure to show her how much he loved her.

I let little girl down

In my career, I've grown accustomed to witnessing the unfortunate, to seeing people pass away. Over time, I sort of became numb to reality—a defense mechanism, I suppose, to deal with the constant exposure to loss and suffering. But when my grandparents passed away, all that numbness was stripped away, and I was brought back to my senses. I remember crying at both of their funerals, something I hadn't done in years. It was as if I had been transported back in time, back to being a nine-year-old boy, watching helplessly as his beloved grandparents were lowered into the ground.

My wife was there for me, as she always has been, standing by my side along with our children. But the loss hit my mother the hardest. Those were her parents, the people who had raised her, and now they were gone. She had already suffered the loss of my father two years prior, and I was terrified of losing her next. Watching her grief unfold, I was reminded of the fleeting nature of life, how quickly time slips away, and how death has a way of making you grip reality with both hands, forcing you to confront the inevitable truth that we are only here for a short while.

As time passed, the weight of these losses began to affect me more than I realized. At work, where I usually maintained a strong professional demeanor, I started to feel cracks forming in my resolve. It was as though the armor I had built around myself, the emotional distance I relied on to get through the day, was beginning to weaken. Then, one day, something happened that broke me in a way I never expected.

I was working in the hospital, and a routine operation had gone wrong. Despite my best efforts, the patient—a grandfather—didn't make it. I was the one who had to deliver the devastating news to the family, a responsibility that never gets easier, no matter how many times you do it. The patient's son and daughter-in-law were there, and I could see the worry in their eyes, the way they held each other's hands as I approached them. I gently but directly explained what had happened, that we had done everything we could, but he hadn't survived the operation.

Just as I was delivering the news, a little girl, who must have been about seven years old, emerged from the bathroom in the patient's room. I hadn't even realized she was there. She overheard my words and, in an instant, her world came crashing down. She let out a heartbreaking cry for her "Pop-Pop," her face crumpling as tears streamed down her cheeks. She ran to her parents, clinging to them as though holding on would somehow bring him back.

In that moment, I felt the full weight of failure. I knew there was nothing more I could have done—medically, we had tried everything. But standing there, watching this little girl's heart shatter, I felt as if I had let her down, as if I had failed her in the worst possible way. Her cries echoed in my mind, louder than any other sound in that hospital, drowning out the sterile beeps and hums of the medical equipment. For the first time in a long time, I was nearly in tears myself.

Usually, I'm able to handle these situations with a level of detachment, not in a cold or unfeeling way, but with a professional approach that allows me to deliver the news gently yet firmly. I've always believed that it's important to be direct about the unfortunate outcome, to give families the truth with compassion. But this time, I wasn't myself. My emotions, which I had kept in check for so long, began to seep through the cracks. I felt raw, vulnerable, and utterly human in a way I hadn't in years.

The grief of that little girl, combined with my own unresolved emotions over the loss of my grandparents, overwhelmed me. It was as if all the sorrow I had pushed aside, all the pain I had refused to acknowledge, came rushing to the surface. I realized then that I needed to take some time away from work, to step back and allow myself to process everything

My promise to my wife

So much was going on at work. I was depressed, my anxiety weighing heavily on me. Some patients weren't making it, and the stress was getting to me. Then, on top of that, I would come home frustrated, particularly because of a pet peeve of mine that I would complain about all the time—I hated coming home with no dinner on the table. After a long, grueling day at work, I would walk into the house expecting to be greeted by a warm meal, only to find nothing. It made me furious.

The house would be clean, the children would be asleep, and my wife, Sara, would be stretched out on the couch, asleep as if she were the one who had worked a 12-hour shift. I would stand there, confused and very upset, staring at her peaceful face. My frustration would boil over. "Hey! Are you gonna get up?" I yelled, startling her awake. She jumped up, quickly fixing her clothes and trying to put her hands on my shoulders to give me a hug, but I pushed her away.

"I'm hungry," I said coldly. "Are you going to fix me something to eat, or do I have to order out? I could've gotten food at the hospital café if I had known you were going to be asleep when I got home, with no meal on the table."

She wiped her face, her eyes still heavy with sleep, and without missing a beat, walked into the kitchen. "What would you like to eat, baby? I'll fix it for you. How was your day?"

Her calm, modest response only made me angrier. How could she be so kind when I was so obviously upset? "You know, a nice T-bone steak with rice would do just fine," I snapped.

"Yes, dear," she said softly, her voice never wavering. I could hear her in the kitchen, struggling to pull the frozen steaks from the back of the freezer.

I went upstairs while she was cooking, my irritation still simmering. When I walked into our bedroom, I saw freshly folded pajamas neatly placed next to my pillow, with my slippers set perfectly beside the bed. The sight should have warmed my heart, but instead, I felt nothing but a mixture of guilt and stubborn pride. I deserved this, I told myself. After all, I had a hard day at work. I deserved to be treated like a king when I walked through the door.

I picked up the pajamas, heading to the bathroom to take a shower. When I turned on the hot water, it was cold. My patience, already thin, snapped. I knew the water was cold because she was running the hot water downstairs in the kitchen. This wasn't the first time this had happened, but today it was too much for me to handle.

"Can you hurry up with the water? Are you washing the dishes yet? Come on!" I yelled down the stairs, my voice echoing in the empty hallway. Finally, the water turned hot, and I quickly washed up. Just as I was about to enjoy the warm water, I heard a little knock on the bathroom door.

"Who is it?" I grumbled, already annoyed.

"It's me, Dad," came the small voice of one of my sons. "Can I use the bathroom, please?"

I sighed, the frustration mounting. "Alright, I'm coming out in a couple of seconds," I said, trying to keep my voice calm. I quickly turned off the shower, wrapped a towel around myself, and stepped out, trying not to drip water on the rug. My mood was worsening by the second.

I barely had time to finish drying myself off before I was rushed out of the bathroom. I was already upset from not having food on the table when I got home, and now this? It just wasn't my day, I thought to myself.

My son came out of the bathroom, smiling up at me. "Hi, Dad! I missed you today. How was work?"

I forced a smile, trying to hide my irritation. "I missed you too, son. Work was work," I said, my tone flat. I asked him, "How were your studies? Did your mom teach you everything you were supposed to learn today?"

He nodded enthusiastically. "Yes, Dad!"

"Good," I said, giving him a quick pat on the head. "I'm going to need you to leave now so I can finish getting dressed, okay?"

"Okay, Dad," he said, closing the door behind him as he left.

I snatched the towel off, pulled on my pajamas, and slipped my feet into the slippers. As I made my way down the steps, the smell of onions hit me. I started sneezing, my eyes watering, and I yelled down to Sara, "You didn't tell me you were going to cook onions in the rice!"

"What's the matter?" she called back, concern in her voice.

"Nothing!" I shouted, my frustration bubbling over. "Nothing's the matter. I just didn't know you were going to cook the rice!"

When I entered the kitchen, she was at the stove, her back to me, stirring the pot of rice with gentle, deliberate movements. The smell of the cooking onions still lingered in the air, making my nose twitch. I was about to say something else, but I stopped myself, clenching my fists at my sides. Why was I so angry? I could see she was trying, but all I could feel was this irrational resentment. I hated myself for it, but I couldn't stop.

She turned to me with a small smile, her eyes soft and tired. "It'll be ready soon. Why don't you sit down? I'll bring it to you when it's done."

I wanted to yell at her, to tell her to stop being so damn nice, but the words caught in my throat. Instead, I just nodded and slumped into a chair at the table, my head pounding from the day's stress.

As I sat there, I thought about the day I had at the hospital. The patients who didn't make it, the long hours, the constant pressure—it all felt like it was crushing me. And now, here at home, all I wanted was some peace, some comfort, but I couldn't find it. Not in the clean house, not in my wife's tired smile, not in the smell of cooking food. I felt lost, adrift in my own anger.

Sara served the meal with the same quiet grace she always did, placing the plate in front of me without a word. The steak was perfectly cooked, the rice fluffy and flavorful despite the onions. I should have thanked her, should have told her how much I appreciated it, but I didn't. I just picked up my fork and started eating, my mind still tangled in the mess of my thoughts.

She sat across from me, her own plate untouched, watching me with those tired eyes. "Is it good?" she asked, her voice soft.

"It's fine," I muttered, not looking up. I couldn't bring myself to meet her gaze, couldn't stand the concern I knew I'd see there.

After dinner, I went back upstairs, leaving Sara to clean up. I collapsed onto the bed, staring up at the ceiling. My mind raced with all the things I wanted to say but couldn't. I knew I was being unfair, that I was taking out my frustrations on the one person who didn't deserve it, but I felt trapped in this cycle of anger and resentment.

Hours passed, and I was still awake, tossing and turning, unable to find any rest. The house was quiet now, the kids long asleep, and I could hear Sara moving around downstairs, the faint clink of dishes being washed, the soft hum of her voice as she sang quietly to herself. That sound, so familiar and comforting, should have soothed me, but it only deepened the guilt gnawing at my insides.

I remembered the early days of our marriage, how happy we had been, how much I had loved coming home to her. Back then, every meal she made was a feast, every smile a blessing. But now? Now, I was blind to it all, my mind clouded by the stress and pressure of a job that was slowly killing me.

It wasn't her fault. I knew that. She hadn't changed. I had.

Finally, unable to take it any longer, I got out of bed and went downstairs. She was in the living room, curled up on the couch, a book in her hands. She looked up when she saw me, her eyes widening in surprise.

"Is everything okay?" she asked, setting the book aside.

I didn't answer right away. I just stood there, staring at her, this woman who had given me everything, who had put up with all my moods, my anger, my neglect, and never once complained. I felt a lump in my throat, the weight of all my guilt pressing down on me.

"I'm sorry," I said finally, my voice barely above a whisper.

Her brow furrowed in confusion. "For what?"

"For everything," I said, my voice breaking. "For being such a jerk. For not appreciating you. For taking out all my anger on you when you didn't deserve it."

She got up and walked over to me, her hand reaching out to touch my arm. "You've had a lot on your plate," she said gently. "I understand."

"No, you don't," I said, shaking my head. "You don't deserve this. You deserve so much better."

She smiled then, a small, sad smile that broke my heart. "Maybe. But I chose you, remember? And I'll keep choosing you, every day, even when it's hard."

I stared at her, the tears that had been threatening to spill over finally breaking free. "Why?" I asked, my voice cracking under the weight of my emotions. "Why do you stay? Why do you keep putting up with me when all I do is hurt you?"

She sighed softly, her hand still resting on my arm, her touch warm and comforting. "Because I love you, Abbott. And because I know that this isn't you. The man I married is still in there somewhere, buried beneath all that anger and pain. I just need you to find him again."

Her words hit me like a freight train. All this time, I'd been blaming her, blaming my job, blaming everything and everyone except the one person who was really at fault—myself. I'd let the stress of my work, the weight of my responsibilities, and the ghosts of my past transform me into someone I didn't even recognize. But deep down, I knew she was right. The man she fell in love with was still inside me, desperately clawing his way to the surface.

"I don't know if I can do it," I admitted, my voice trembling. "I don't know if I can be that man again."

"You don't have to do it alone," she said softly, her eyes filled with a tenderness that I didn't deserve. "We'll figure it out together. But you have to let me in. You have to talk to me, tell me what's going on inside that head of yours."

I nodded, swallowing hard as I tried to keep my composure. I didn't deserve her kindness, her understanding, but here she was, offering it to me anyway. "I'm so sorry, Sara," I whispered, my voice thick with emotion. "I'm sorry for everything. I promise I'll do better. I'll be better."

She smiled again, this time a genuine, warm smile that reached her eyes. "I believe you," she said simply. "But it's going to take time. And that's okay. We've got time."

I pulled her into my arms, holding her close as the weight of everything I'd been carrying finally started to lift. She felt so small and fragile in my embrace, but at the same time, I realized how strong she truly was. She had carried us both for so long, and now it was my turn to shoulder the burden, to step up and be the man she needed me to be.

We stood there for what felt like an eternity, wrapped in each other's arms, the silence between us filled with unspoken promises and a renewed sense of hope. I knew the road ahead wouldn't be easy. There would be days when I would stumble, when the anger and frustration would try to creep back in. But I also knew that with Sara by my side, I could overcome anything.

That night, for the first time in a long time, I slept peacefully. No nightmares, no tossing and turning, just the steady rhythm of Sara's breathing beside me, grounding me in the present, reminding me of what truly mattered.

The next morning, I woke up before the sun, the house still shrouded in darkness. I slipped out of bed quietly, not wanting to wake Sara, and made my way downstairs. The kitchen was still warm from the night before, the faint smell of onions lingering in the air. I decided to make breakfast, something simple—eggs, toast, and coffee. As I cooked, I thought about the conversation we'd had the night before, about the promises I'd made and the changes I knew I needed to make.

I was halfway through frying the eggs when I heard footsteps behind me. I turned to see Sara standing in the doorway, her hair tousled from sleep, her eyes soft with the remnants of dreams.

"You're up early," she said, a hint of surprise in her voice.

"Yeah," I replied, turning back to the stove. "I thought I'd make us some breakfast."

She walked over to me, peeking over my shoulder at the pan. "Smells good," she said, her voice filled with warmth.

"It's just eggs," I said with a small smile, flipping the eggs in the pan.

"Even so," she said, leaning against the counter. "Thank you."

We sat down to eat together, the morning light slowly filtering through the kitchen windows, casting a soft glow on everything it touched. It was a simple meal, but it felt like a new beginning, a small step toward the life we both wanted. We didn't talk much as we ate, but the silence between us was comfortable, a quiet understanding that words weren't necessary.

After breakfast, I offered to clean up, but Sara insisted on helping. We worked side by side, washing dishes and wiping down counters, a routine we had done countless times before but that now felt different—more meaningful, more connected.

As the days passed, I made a conscious effort to keep the promises I had made to Sara that night. I started to talk more openly with her, sharing my thoughts, my fears, and my struggles instead of bottling them up inside. I learned to recognize the signs of my frustration before they boiled over and found healthier ways to cope with the stress that came from work.

It wasn't easy. There were days when I felt like I was slipping back into old habits, when the weight of everything seemed too much to bear. But every time I started to falter, I remembered that moment in the kitchen, the warmth of Sara's embrace, and the promise I had made to be better—not just for her, but for myself as well.

Sara was patient with me, always there with a kind word or a gentle touch whenever I needed it. She never pushed, never demanded more than I could give, but I could see the relief in her eyes, the hope that had been missing for so long slowly returning.

Over time, our relationship began to heal. We started going out again, rekindling the spark that had first brought us together all those years ago. We laughed more, talked more, and the house, once filled with tension, was now filled with the sound of our voices, the laughter of our children, and the warmth of a love that had been tested but had ultimately endured.

One evening, after putting the kids to bed, we found ourselves sitting on the porch, watching the sun set over the horizon. The sky was painted in shades of pink and orange, the world bathed in the soft glow of twilight. Sara leaned her head on my shoulder, and I wrapped my arm around her, pulling her close.

"Remember when we used to do this all the time?" she asked, her voice soft and nostalgic.

"Yeah," I replied, my voice filled with the same nostalgia. "We'd sit out here for hours, just talking about everything and nothing."

She smiled, a contented sigh escaping her lips. "I've missed this," she said.

"Me too," I admitted, pressing a kiss to the top of her head.

We sat there in comfortable silence, the weight of the past slowly fading away, replaced by the quiet contentment of the present. For the first time in a long time, I felt at peace, not just with Sara, but with myself.

That night, as we lay in bed, I held her close, the steady rhythm of her breathing lulling me to sleep. I knew that the road ahead would still have its challenges, that there would be moments of doubt and fear, but I also knew that as long as we faced them together, we could overcome anything.

In the end, it wasn't about grand gestures or sweeping declarations of love. It was about the little things—the quiet moments shared, the small acts of kindness, and the unwavering commitment to each other, even when things got tough. It was about choosing to love, every single day, even when it wasn't easy.

And as I drifted off to sleep, with Sara's warm body pressed against mine, I realized that I had finally found my way back to the man I used to be—the man she had fallen in love with all those years ago. And I knew that as long as I kept choosing her, just as she had always chosen me, we would be okay

The importance of working on your marriage

I sat in my study seat, the soft glow of the desk lamp casting a warm light over the papers scattered across my desk. I had always found solace in this room, a quiet space where I could think, reflect, and, lately, write. The events of the past few months had left me with much to ponder, and I felt compelled to capture my thoughts on the unique and sacred bond that marriage represented, not only in my life but in the lives of so many others.

I picked up my pen and began to write, the words flowing from a place deep within me, where love, regret, faith, and hope intertwined.

Marriage is not merely a contract between two individuals; it is a covenant, an inviolable bond that fuses two souls into a union that transcends the corporeal and ascends into the spiritual realm. This relationship, when meticulously nurtured and reverently cherished, evolves into a wellspring of immeasurable fortitude, profound joy, and unparalleled fulfillment. Yet, like all things of immense worth, it demands unwavering effort, resolute commitment, and, above all, an abiding and transcendent love.

When I first met Sara, I was struck by her kindness, her intelligence, and the way her eyes lit up when she laughed. There was a connection between us that I couldn't quite explain, something that went beyond the surface. It was as if our souls recognized each other, and we were drawn together by an invisible force that neither of us could resist. I knew, even in those early days, that she was the one I wanted to spend my life with.

But marriage, I soon learned, is not simply about finding someone you love and deciding to spend your life with them. It is about choosing that person every single day, even when things are difficult, even when life throws challenges your way that you never saw coming. It is about building a life together, brick by brick, moment by moment, with each act of kindness, each word of encouragement, and each shared experience adding to the foundation of your relationship.

One of the most profound lessons I've learned in my marriage is the importance of communication. It seems so simple, so obvious, but it is often the most overlooked aspect of a relationship. We assume that our partner knows what we're thinking, what we're feeling, or that they should understand us without needing to explain ourselves. But this is a dangerous assumption, one that can lead to misunderstandings, resentment, and, ultimately, distance.

Sara and I fell into this trap early in our marriage. I was so focused on my career, on providing for our family, that I neglected the emotional needs of our relationship. I assumed that as long as I was working hard and bringing home a paycheck, everything else would fall into place. But marriage is not a business transaction; it is a partnership, a union that requires both partners to be fully present, fully engaged.

There were times when I would come home, exhausted from a long day at the hospital, and I would find Sara waiting for me, eager to share the events of her day, to connect with me on a deeper level. But I was too tired, too distracted, to truly listen. I would nod, offer a few words of encouragement, but my mind was elsewhere, thinking about the patients I couldn't save, the surgeries that didn't go as planned. I didn't realize then how much this hurt her, how much she needed me to be present, to truly see her and hear her.Marriage is a journey, not a destination. It's easy to think that once the wedding bells have chimed and the vows have been exchanged, the hard work is over. But in truth, the real work begins the moment you say "I do." A successful marriage requires continuous effort, a commitment to growth, and an unwavering resolve to be the best version of yourself, not just for your spouse, but for the relationship as a whole.

The importance of working on your marriage cannot be overstated. It's tempting to get comfortable, to let the daily grind take over, and to assume that everything will fall into place naturally. However, marriage, like any valuable endeavor, demands consistent attention and nurturing. It's about making a conscious decision every day to invest in your relationship, to show up with love, kindness, and a willingness to communicate, even when it's difficult.

One of the keys to a lasting marriage is the recognition that neither you nor your spouse is perfect. We all have flaws, shortcomings, and moments of weakness. Acknowledging this is crucial because it allows you to approach your relationship with humility and grace. Understanding that you're not perfect helps you to be more forgiving of your partner's mistakes, and it also challenges you to keep striving for personal growth.

Being the best version of yourself in a marriage doesn't mean being flawless. Rather, it means making a consistent effort to improve, to learn from past mistakes, and to approach each day with a fresh perspective. It's about striving to be patient when you're frustrated, to listen when you'd rather speak, and to love unconditionally, even when it's hard. This ongoing self-improvement not only benefits you personally but also strengthens the bond between you and your spouse.

However, striving for improvement doesn't mean you should tolerate being treated poorly, nor should you allow yourself to stoop low intentionally. There's a fine line between being understanding and being taken for granted. It's essential to set boundaries, to communicate openly about your needs and expectations, and to hold yourself and your spouse accountable for maintaining respect and love in the relationship.

In marriage, it's easy to fall into patterns, to let small resentments build up, and to find yourself drifting apart without even realizing it. This is why it's so important to never give up on working on your marriage. Regular check-ins, honest conversations, and a willingness to address issues head-on are vital. It's about recognizing when things aren't right and having the courage to make the necessary changes before those small issues become insurmountable problems.

Never giving up on your marriage means committing to the long haul, to the ups and downs, and to the understanding that the person you married will change over time, just as you will. It's about embracing those changes, growing together, and finding new ways to connect and strengthen your bond. It's about remembering why you fell in love in the first place and holding on to that, even when life gets tough.

Ultimately, a successful marriage is built on the foundation of two people who are committed to loving each other through all of life's challenges. It's about working together to create a partnership that is rooted in respect, trust, and a shared vision for the future. It's about choosing each other every single day and never losing sight of the importance of that choice.

So, as you continue on your journey together, remember that the work you put into your marriage is an investment in a lifetime of love and companionship. Be patient with yourself and with your partner. Keep striving to be the best version of yourself, and never give up on the love that brought you together in the first place. Because in the end, a marriage that is nurtured and cherished will grow stronger with each passing day, and the rewards of that effort will be immeasurable.

37

I was a bad husband

There was a time in my marriage when I took affection for granted. Life had a way of pulling me in a thousand different directions—my career, the responsibilities of fatherhood, the endless demands of daily life. It wasn't that I didn't love Sara; I loved her deeply. But somewhere along the way, I forgot the importance of showing that love in a tangible, visible way. I assumed that she knew how I felt, that the words "I love you" whispered before bed or the occasional bouquet of flowers were enough. But they weren't. Not for her, and not for the example I wanted to set for our children.

I began to realize that affection is more than just a fleeting expression of love; it is the lifeblood of a marriage. It's the small acts of kindness, the gentle touches, the warm embraces that keep the connection between husband and wife alive and thriving. Affection is the glue that holds a relationship together, especially during the tough times. And for our children, it is a powerful model of what love looks like—an indelible image that they will carry with them into their own relationships.

It started with a simple observation. I noticed how our children would light up when Sara and I shared a moment of affection. Whether it was a quick kiss in the kitchen, holding hands while walking through the park, or just a loving glance exchanged across the room, our children's eyes would follow us, their faces would brighten, and they would often try to mimic what they saw. I realized then that these moments were not just important for Sara and me, but for them as well. They were learning about love, about marriage, and about what it means to be a husband and wife, through the way I treated their mother.

This realization hit me like a wave. I had been so focused on being a provider, on ensuring that our family had everything it needed materially, that I had overlooked the emotional and psychological needs of my wife and children. I understood that I needed to change, to make a conscious effort to show Sara how much I loved and appreciated her—not just for her sake, but for the sake of our children, who were quietly absorbing everything they saw.

Affection is a powerful thing. It's more than just a physical act; it's a way of communicating love without words. A simple touch on the shoulder, a hug after a long day, or a smile shared across a crowded room can convey more than a thousand words ever could. These small gestures are the building blocks of a strong marriage, and they are crucial in maintaining a deep emotional connection.

For Sara, I began to realize, affection was more than just a luxury—it was a necessity. It was how she felt loved, valued, and secure in our marriage. And for me, showing affection became a way to reaffirm my commitment to her, to remind her that she was not just my partner in life, but the love of my life. It became a way to reconnect, to push aside the stress and chaos of everyday life and focus on the bond we shared.

But it was also more than that. Showing affection to Sara had a ripple effect that extended far beyond our relationship. It impacted the entire family dynamic. Our children, who were always watching and learning, began to understand the importance of love and respect in a marriage. They saw firsthand that love wasn't just something you said; it was something you did, something you lived every day.

As a father, I understood that I was not just raising sons; I was raising future husbands and fathers. The way I treated Sara would set the standard for how they would treat their future wives. This was a profound responsibility, one that I didn't take lightly. I wanted my sons to grow up understanding that love was not just a feeling, but an action. That showing affection was not a sign of weakness, but of strength. That being a loving, affectionate husband was one of the most important roles they could ever play.

I started to be more intentional about how I showed affection to Sara, especially in front of our children. I wanted them to see that love is expressed in the little things—holding hands while watching a movie, giving her a kiss on the cheek when I walked in the door, or simply telling her how beautiful she looked. I wanted them to understand that these moments were not just for show, but were genuine expressions of my love and commitment to their mother.

And I noticed a change. Not just in Sara, who seemed more at ease, more content, but in our children as well. They became more affectionate themselves, more loving and considerate. They began to mimic the way I treated Sara, showing her the same respect and care that I did. It was a beautiful thing to see, and it made me realize just how important it was for them to witness our love firsthand.

One of the lessons I've learned is that affection must be consistent. It's easy to show love when things are going well, but the real test of a marriage is how you treat each other when life gets tough. It's during these times that affection is most needed, and yet it's often the first thing to go. Stress, exhaustion, and frustration can make it difficult to reach out to your spouse, to offer a kind word or a loving touch. But these are the moments when affection can make all the difference.

I made a conscious decision to be more consistent in showing affection to Sara, even when I didn't feel like it. Especially when I didn't feel like it. I realized that these were the moments that mattered most—the times when she needed to know that I was still there, still committed, still in love with her despite the challenges we were facing. It wasn't always easy, but it was always worth it.

And in doing so, I was also teaching our children an invaluable lesson. They were learning that love isn't always easy, but it's always worth the effort. They were seeing that marriage is about more than just the good times; it's about sticking together through the hard times, about choosing to love and care for each other even when it's difficult. They were learning that affection isn't just something you do when you feel like it; it's something you do because it's important, because it's what makes a marriage strong.

As our children grew, I could see the impact that my relationship with Sara was having on them. They were becoming more aware of the way I treated her, more attuned to the affection I showed her. And as they grew older, I began to notice something remarkable—they started to model that behavior in their own lives.

Our sons, in particular, began to show a level of respect and consideration for Sara that went beyond mere obedience. They would open doors for her, help her with household tasks without being asked, and always made sure to say "I love you" before going to bed. They were learning, through my example, how to be loving and respectful husbands, even before they fully understood what that meant.

And I knew that when the time came for them to start their own families, they would carry these lessons with them. They would remember the way I treated their mother, the way I showed her love and affection, and they would bring that into their own marriages. They would understand that love is not just a word, but an action. That being a good husband means being affectionate, considerate, and always putting your spouse's needs before your own.

In the end, I realized that showing affection to Sara wasn't just about strengthening our marriage; it was about leaving a legacy for our children. A legacy of love, respect, and commitment that would shape the way they approached their own relationships. It was about teaching them that love is something you show, every day, in big ways and small.

And as I looked at our children, at the way they interacted with Sara and with each other, I knew that I was doing something right. I knew that they were learning the lessons I wanted them to learn—that love is something you work at, something you cherish, and something you show, every day, in every way.

Marriage is not just about the two people in it; it's about the family you create together, the children you raise, and the legacy you leave behind. By showing affection to Sara, I was not just nurturing our relationship; I was nurturing our family, creating a foundation of love and respect that would carry on long after we were gone.

And that, to me, was the most important thing of all.

Words have the power to build up or tear down

The Bible consistently highlights the importance of love, especially within the sanctity of marriage. Ephesians 5:25-28 provides a powerful directive to husbands, calling them to love their wives as Christ loved the Church. This love is not merely an emotion but a deep, sacrificial commitment that reflects the sanctity of marriage. However, the real challenge often lies in the practical application of this divine command. Too often, couples who profess strong Christian beliefs find themselves ensnared in the very behaviors that Scripture warns against, such as using love as a weapon and words as tools for harm. Understanding the profound impact of words within a marriage is critical for avoiding these pitfalls.

The passage in Ephesians 5:25-28 is a profound instruction on how a husband should love his wife. The love described here is not conditional or superficial; it is a love that mirrors Christ's love for the Church—selfless, sacrificial, and purifying. Christ's love for the Church was so profound that He gave Himself up for her, and in doing so, He cleansed and sanctified her. Similarly, husbands are called to love their wives with the same dedication, ensuring that their love is purifying, uplifting, and free from blemish. This love is holistic, encompassing not just the physical and emotional aspects but the spiritual well-being of the wife.

In the context of marriage, words hold incredible power. Proverbs 18:21 (KJV) states, "Death and life are in the power of the tongue: and they that love it shall eat the fruit thereof." This verse emphasizes that words can either build up or tear down, bringing life or death to a relationship. When spoken in love, words can heal, encourage, and strengthen the bond between husband and wife. However, when words are spoken in anger, frustration, or malice, they can inflict deep emotional wounds that may take years to heal.

In the heat of an argument, it can be easy to forget the weight that our words carry. What might seem like a fleeting moment of anger or frustration can leave lasting scars on the mind and heart of the person we love. Verbal abuse is not always recognized immediately, but it is insidious and can slowly erode the trust and love that are the foundations of a healthy marriage. Over time, the accumulation of hurtful words can lead to resentment, bitterness, and a sense of hopelessness in the relationship.

Verbal abuse in marriage is often downplayed or misunderstood. It does not always manifest as overtly harsh or cruel language. Sometimes, it can be subtle, disguised as sarcasm, passive-aggressive comments, or constant criticism. However, regardless of how it is delivered, verbal abuse is damaging because it attacks the person's self-worth and dignity. The effects of verbal abuse are not just emotional; they can also have a profound impact on a person's mental and physical health.

The brain is particularly susceptible to the effects of verbal abuse. Research has shown that the brain processes emotional pain in a similar way to physical pain. Words that are meant to harm trigger the same areas of the brain that respond to physical injury, meaning that emotional wounds can be just as painful and long-lasting as physical ones. This is why verbal abuse can leave "scars" on the brain, altering how a person perceives themselves and their relationship.

When we speak, our words are processed by the brain, which then assigns meaning to them based on context, tone, and intent. Positive words, such as those that express love, encouragement, and support, activate the brain's reward system, releasing chemicals like dopamine and oxytocin, which promote feelings of happiness, trust, and connection. This is why affirmations, compliments, and kind words can strengthen a marriage, creating a positive feedback loop that fosters intimacy and closeness.

On the other hand, negative words, especially those spoken in anger or with the intent to hurt, activate the brain's stress response. This triggers the release of stress hormones like cortisol, which, in high levels, can have detrimental effects on the brain and body. Chronic exposure to negative language can lead to anxiety, depression, and a host of physical ailments, including high blood pressure, heart disease, and weakened immune function. The brain, when subjected to consistent verbal abuse, may also begin to rewire itself, leading to changes in how a person thinks, feels, and behaves. This can manifest as low self-esteem, difficulty trusting others, and an increased risk of developing mental health disorders.

Ephesians 5:25-28 not only calls husbands to love their wives but also to do so in a way that is pure and selfless. Love, in its truest form, is never used as a weapon. However, when one partner begins to withhold love, affection, or kindness as a form of punishment or control, they are essentially weaponizing love. This is a grave sin because it distorts the very nature of love and undermines the purpose of marriage.

When love is used as a weapon, it creates a dynamic of power and control, where one partner seeks to dominate the other. This is contrary to the biblical model of marriage, which is based on mutual respect, submission, and love. Ephesians 5:21 (KJV) states, "Submitting yourselves one to another in the fear of God." This verse highlights that both partners are called to submit to each other out of reverence for God, not to seek control or dominance over one another.

It is not enough for Christian couples to simply hear the word of God; they must also be doers of the word. James 1:22 (KJV) admonishes, "But be ye doers of the word, and not hearers only, deceiving your own selves." This means that couples must actively strive to live out the principles of love, kindness, and respect in their daily interactions. They must be vigilant in guarding their tongues and ensuring that their words align with the teachings of Christ.

When conflicts arise, as they inevitably will in any marriage, couples should remember the power of their words and choose to speak life rather than death into their relationship. This requires humility, self-control, and a commitment to the well-being of the other person. It means being quick to listen, slow to speak, and slow to anger (James 1:19), recognizing that words spoken in anger can cause irreparable damage.

Ephesians 5:25-28 offers a blueprint for a Christ-centered marriage, one that is built on the foundation of selfless, sacrificial love. For a marriage to thrive, both partners must be committed to loving each other as Christ loved the Church, with a love that is pure, uplifting, and free from blemish. This requires not only a deep understanding of the power of words but also a commitment to using them wisely and lovingly.

Words have the power to build up or tear down, to heal or to hurt. In marriage, where the bond is sacred and the stakes are high, couples must be especially mindful of the words they speak. By choosing to speak words of love, encouragement, and affirmation, couples can strengthen their bond and create a marriage that reflects the love of Christ. Conversely, by avoiding words spoken in anger or malice, they can protect their relationship from the destructive effects of verbal abuse. In doing so, they fulfill the biblical mandate to love each other as Christ loved the Church, creating a marriage that is truly holy and without blemish.

Growth and Learning

In my younger days as a husband, my approach to marriage was profoundly flawed. My understanding of what it meant to be a provider was narrow and misguided. I believed that my primary responsibility was financial—that if I worked hard, earned money, and provided materially, I was fulfilling my role as a husband. This perspective, however, was both incomplete and detrimental to our relationship.

At that time, I viewed financial provision as the cornerstone of my duties. When Sara would express a desire to go somewhere or do something that involved spending money, I would react with irritation and frustration. My response was disproportionate, rooted in a belief that her requests were a burden on our finances, rather than a reflection of her needs and desires. I didn't recognize that my anger was a direct consequence of my own choices and misjudgments.

The root of this frustration was the decision I had made to have Sara quit her job. I convinced her to leave her position because I believed it would make her happier, less stressed, and more fulfilled. I thought that as a Christian husband, I should be the sole provider and that this would be in line with my spiritual duties. Yet, in my pursuit to align with what I thought was a godly husband's role, I overlooked a critical aspect: I was still embodying a worldly mindset, consumed by my own selfish needs and desires.

I had convinced myself that by being the sole financial provider, I was fulfilling my responsibilities. I took pride in this role, viewing it as a testament to my commitment to our marriage and my faith. However, I failed to see that being a provider extends beyond financial contributions. It encompasses spiritual, physical, and emotional dimensions, all of which are essential for a balanced and nurturing relationship.

Financial provision is indeed important, but it is only one facet of a holistic approach to being a husband. True provision involves much more than just bringing home a paycheck. It means being present in every aspect of your wife's life, supporting her not only materially but also emotionally and spiritually. It requires an understanding that being a Christian man means serving your wife in all areas, embodying love, patience, and selflessness.

Spiritually, a husband's role is to be a guide and a partner in faith. This involves leading by example, nurturing a shared spiritual life, and providing encouragement and support in times of spiritual struggle. It's about creating a home where faith is central, where both partners grow together in their understanding of God and His teachings. I failed in this regard, as my focus was primarily on material provision, leaving little room for spiritual connection and growth.

Physically, a husband is called to be a source of strength and support. This means being attentive to your wife's needs, offering comfort and care, and participating actively in the life you are building together. It's about being a partner in every aspect of daily life, from handling chores and responsibilities to providing emotional and physical support during challenging times. My younger self had much to learn about this dimension, as my view was limited to financial contributions without acknowledging the need for physical and emotional presence.

Mentally, being a provider involves emotional intelligence and empathy. It requires understanding your wife's feelings, being responsive to her needs, and offering support when she is struggling. I had not fully grasped this aspect, often reacting with frustration rather than compassion when Sara expressed her needs or desires. I failed to realize that my reactions were indicative of a deeper issue—my own struggle with control and self-centeredness, rather than a true understanding of partnership and support.

In retrospect, I see now how my approach was misguided. I allowed my own insecurities and misconceptions to dictate my behavior, leading to conflicts and misunderstandings. I was focused on fulfilling a role that I believed was aligned with my faith, but I neglected the broader, more nuanced responsibilities of a husband. I didn't recognize that my role was not just to provide financially, but to offer a comprehensive form of support that included spiritual guidance, physical presence, and emotional understanding.

My journey has been one of growth and learning. I have come to understand that being a provider is not about asserting control or prioritizing financial contributions above all else. It is about being a balanced, loving, and supportive partner in every aspect of life. It's about embodying the values of faith, love, and commitment in a way that encompasses all dimensions of marriage.

As Christian men, we are called to model a holistic approach to being a husband—one that integrates financial, spiritual, physical, and emotional support. This understanding has transformed my approach to marriage, guiding me to be a more attentive, compassionate, and supportive partner. It's a journey of continual growth and reflection, one that requires a willingness to learn from past mistakes and to strive for a more profound understanding of what it means to truly serve and love one's spouse.

In this journey, I have come to appreciate the depth and breadth of my role as a husband. It's not just about meeting financial needs, but about fostering a loving, supportive, and spiritually enriching relationship. By embracing this comprehensive approach, I have been able to build a stronger, more meaningful connection with Sara and create a positive example for our children—a testament to the power of genuine, multifaceted love and commitment in a marriage.

Embodying the principles of love

The concept of servitude in Christian doctrine often evokes images of submission and duty, but it is essential to understand that this servitude is not about enforcing control or dominance over others. Instead, as Christians, our role as servants is deeply intertwined with our commitment to love, honor, and respect each other. This perspective transforms servitude from a burdensome obligation into a profound expression of mutual support and divine purpose.

To be a servant in the Christian context means to embody the teachings and example set forth by Jesus Christ. Jesus, the Son of God, exemplified servitude not through authority but through humility and service to others. In John 13:12-15, Jesus washed His disciples' feet, an act that was both physically and culturally significant in demonstrating His commitment to serve rather than to be served. This act of washing feet, which was typically performed by the lowest of servants, was a radical statement about the nature of leadership and service in the Kingdom of

God.

Jesus' teachings emphasize that true greatness comes not from wielding power over others but from serving them. In Matthew 20:26-28, Jesus declares, "Whoever wants to become great among you must be your servant, and whoever wants to be first must be your slave—just as the Son of Man did not come to be served, but to serve, and to give his life as a ransom for many." This principle applies to all aspects of Christian life, including marriage.

In marriage, being a servant does not imply that one partner is subordinate to the other. Instead, it means that both husband and wife are called to serve each other with love, respect, and selflessness. Ephesians 5:21 says, "Submit to one another out of reverence for Christ." This mutual submission is not about dominance or inequality but about honoring and serving each other in the context of a loving and supportive partnership.

For husbands, serving their wives involves loving them as Christ loved the Church. Ephesians 5:25 instructs, "Husbands, love your wives, just as Christ loved the Church and gave himself up for her." This sacrificial love requires putting the needs of one's wife above one's own, being attentive to her emotional and physical needs, and supporting her in her personal and spiritual growth. It means being a source of strength and encouragement, not only in times of joy but also during hardships.

For wives, serving their husbands means showing respect and supporting them as they fulfill their role as spiritual leaders of the household. Ephesians 5:22-24 encourages wives to submit to their husbands as to the Lord, recognizing their role in fostering a harmonious and loving relationship. This submission is not about relinquishing personal identity or values but about working together in unity and purpose.

Being a servant in the Christian sense also involves understanding that our service is ultimately to God. Colossians 3:23-24 states, "Whatever you do, work at it with all your heart, as working for the Lord, not for human masters, since you know that you will receive an inheritance from the Lord as a reward. It is the Lord Christ you are serving." This perspective shifts the focus from mere human expectations to divine fulfillment. When we serve our spouses and others, we are acting in obedience to God's commandments and reflecting His love and grace.

In marriage, servitude means creating a relationship where both partners are committed to uplifting and supporting one another. This involves practical acts of service as well as emotional and spiritual support. It requires active listening, empathy, and a willingness to put the other's needs first, even when it requires personal sacrifice.

Practical acts of service might include sharing household responsibilities, supporting each other's careers and personal ambitions, and taking time to nurture the relationship through quality time and communication. Emotional support involves being present during times of stress or difficulty, offering encouragement and reassurance, and being a steadfast companion through life's ups and downs.

Spiritually, servitude in marriage means praying together, seeking God's guidance in making decisions, and growing together in faith. It involves encouraging each other's spiritual development, studying Scripture together, and engaging in activities that strengthen the marital bond and the relationship with God.

Serving one's spouse can be challenging, especially in times of conflict or disagreement. However, the Christian call to servitude encourages us to approach these challenges with a spirit of humility and grace. James 1:19 advises, "Everyone should be quick to listen, slow to speak and slow to become angry." This approach fosters healthy communication and conflict resolution, allowing both partners to feel heard and valued.

Servitude also involves forgiveness and reconciliation. Colossians 3:13 urges, "Bear with each other and forgive one another if any of you has a grievance against someone. Forgive as the Lord forgave you." In a marriage, this means letting go of grudges, seeking forgiveness when needed, and working towards healing and restoration in the relationship.

When both partners embrace the role of servant-leaders in their marriage, the relationship becomes a reflection of Christ's love and grace. This dynamic creates a supportive and nurturing environment where both individuals can thrive and grow. It transforms the marriage into a partnership where mutual respect, love, and commitment are the cornerstones.

Moreover, this approach to marriage sets a powerful example

for others, particularly for children. When children witness their parents serving and loving each other selflessly, they learn valuable lessons about relationships, respect, and faith. These lessons can shape their understanding of marriage and influence how they approach their own relationships in the future.

Understanding and embracing the role of a servant in marriage involves a shift in perspective. It requires moving beyond traditional notions of dominance and control and embracing a model of mutual support and divine purpose. By serving our spouses with love, respect, and selflessness, we fulfill our Christian calling and build a marriage that reflects the teachings of Christ.

In conclusion, being a servant as a Christian means more than fulfilling obligations or adhering to societal roles. It involves embodying the principles of love, humility, and grace in our interactions with others. In marriage, this means serving each other with a spirit of devotion and respect, grounded in our commitment to God. By doing so, we create a relationship that honors God and reflects His love, strength, and compassion.

Before Anything

I n life, we are presented with two distinct paths: the positive and the negative. Each choice we make aligns us with one path or the other, and our journey through life is defined by these decisions. As Christians, we are called to embody the principles of our faith in all aspects of our lives, including our personal development. Recognizing a need for change within oneself is a profound moment of self-awareness that offers an opportunity for growth and transformation. This chapter explores why it is crucial to embrace change and how this commitment aligns with our spiritual obligations.

The journey of self-improvement begins with an honest assessment of our behavior, attitudes, and values. When we acknowledge areas in our lives that require change, we embark on a path of personal growth that reflects our dedication to serving God. This recognition is not merely about altering superficial aspects of our behavior but involves a deeper, more meaningful transformation that aligns with our spiritual calling.

As Christians, our primary obligation is to serve Christ with unwavering commitment. This service is not confined to specific aspects of our lives but extends to every area, including our professional careers, relationships, and personal conduct. It is a holistic approach that demands we integrate our faith into our daily lives and make choices that reflect our dedication to God's teachings. The recognition of a need for change is an essential step in this process, as it signifies our willingness to align ourselves more closely with Christ's example.

Acknowledging the need for change often requires confronting uncomfortable truths about ourselves. This can be a challenging process, as it involves examining our behaviors, attitudes, and motivations with a critical eye. However, this self-examination is vital for spiritual growth and transformation. When we recognize areas where we fall short of our spiritual ideals, we are presented with an opportunity to make deliberate changes that enhance our alignment with God's will.

The importance of making these changes lies in our commitment to living a life that reflects Christ's teachings. The decisions we make and the way we conduct ourselves are manifestations of our faith. By choosing to address and improve upon our shortcomings, we demonstrate our dedication to embodying the principles of love, compassion, and integrity that Christ exemplified. This commitment to change is not just a personal endeavor but a testament to our spiritual journey and our desire to serve God faithfully.

In our professional careers, this commitment to change and growth is equally significant. Regardless of the field we work in or the region of the world we inhabit, our actions and choices should reflect our Christian values. This means conducting ourselves with honesty, integrity, and respect, and striving to make a positive impact through our work. When we approach our careers with a mindset of service and dedication to Christ, we transform our professional lives into an extension of our spiritual practice.

This commitment to change also has implications for our interactions with others. Our relationships with family, friends, and colleagues provide opportunities to demonstrate the love and grace of Christ. By addressing our own areas of improvement and striving to embody Christ's teachings, we set an example for others and create a positive influence in our communities. This holistic approach to living out our faith reinforces the idea that our service to God is not limited to specific contexts but permeates every aspect of our lives.

Embracing change and committing to personal growth also involves seeking guidance and support from God. Prayer, reflection, and seeking counsel from spiritual mentors are crucial components of this process. By turning to God for strength and wisdom, we align ourselves with His guidance and gain the clarity needed to navigate the path of transformation. This spiritual support reinforces our commitment to change and helps us remain focused on our ultimate goal of serving Christ faithfully.

Moreover, recognizing the need for change and taking action demonstrates humility and a willingness to grow. It acknowledges that we are not perfect and that our journey of faith involves continuous learning and development. This humility is an essential aspect of Christian living, as it reflects our understanding of our dependence on God and our commitment to becoming better reflections of His love and grace.

Again recognizing a need for change within ourselves is a pivotal moment in our spiritual journey. It signifies a willingness to align our lives more closely with Christ's teachings and to embody our faith in all aspects of our existence. By embracing this opportunity for growth and transformation, we reaffirm our commitment to serving God with dedication and integrity. Whether in our personal lives, professional careers, or interactions with others, this commitment to change reflects our dedication to living out our faith and serving Christ faithfully.

Understanding relationship

I made a grave error in my understanding of marriage. For a long time, I believed that my wife's unwavering willingness to meet my every need stemmed from my financial contributions or from the conventional notion that a man should be served by his wife. I was mistaken. Her dedication had little to do with her role as a woman or my role as a man. Instead, it was rooted in something much deeper— her commitment to serving God and honoring the promise she made before Him.

I had been living under the illusion that her actions were motivated by the material aspects of our life or by societal expectations. However, this misconception overshadowed a more profound truth: her devotion to our marriage was fundamentally connected to her relationship with God. It was her faith, not any earthly consideration, that inspired her to persevere and serve with unconditional love.

In retrospect, I can see now that my wife's commitment to our marriage was more than just a fulfillment of a marital obligation; it was an act of spiritual devotion. Her adherence to the teachings of the Bible and her promise to stand by me through all circumstances—good and bad—was a testament to her spiritual integrity. This commitment was not contingent on my behavior or the financial stability of our household but was instead a reflection of her relationship with God.

If she had acted solely on her human desires and perceptions, it's likely our marriage would have ended long ago. Her commitment to God kept her bound to me even when my actions and attitudes fell short of what was expected in a marriage. Her spiritual connection provided a foundation strong enough to withstand the turbulent times and imperfections that marred our journey together.

It is crucial to understand that a relationship with God is indispensable in a marriage. Financial stability, physical appearance, and even our earthly possessions are transient and subject to change. Money can fluctuate, age can alter our physical capabilities, and even our bodies will eventually succumb to the ravages of time. Yet, a relationship with God remains constant, unchanging, and eternal.

When we place our trust and reliance on material aspects or societal roles, we overlook the profound spiritual dimensions that sustain a marriage. The essence of a strong marital bond is not rooted in the transient elements of life but in a deep, unwavering connection with God. This divine relationship provides the strength to navigate the inevitable challenges that arise and ensures that our commitment to one another transcends the superficial aspects of our existence.

In the context of marriage, this divine connection is vital. It shapes how we interact with one another, how we respond to each other's needs, and how we handle conflict. A relationship grounded in faith fosters a sense of purpose and direction that surpasses earthly concerns. It provides a framework for understanding and compassion that can weather any storm.

Moreover, a deep spiritual connection influences how we view our roles within the marriage. It encourages us to serve one another with genuine love and selflessness, mirroring the divine love that God shows us. This service is not driven by obligation or societal expectations but by a heartfelt commitment to honor God's teachings and to support our partner in every aspect of their life.

Reflecting on my own shortcomings, I realize how my failure to recognize this spiritual dimension led to misunderstandings and frustrations. I expected my wife's service to be a direct reflection of my contributions and societal norms, rather than acknowledging the spiritual depth of her commitment. This perspective was flawed and failed to appreciate the true essence of her devotion.

Understanding that my wife's dedication was a reflection of her faith rather than just a response to my actions has reshaped my approach to our marriage. It has illuminated the importance of nurturing our spiritual relationship and recognizing that our commitment to each other is intertwined with our commitment to God. This realization has encouraged me to reevaluate my role in our marriage and to strive to embody the principles of love, patience, and humility that God exemplifies.

As we move forward, it is essential to prioritize our relationship with God as the cornerstone of our marriage. This spiritual foundation will guide us through challenges, help us grow together, and sustain our commitment to one another. By focusing on our divine connection, we can build a marriage that is not only resilient but also deeply fulfilling.

In conclusion, the true essence of a lasting and meaningful marriage lies in the strength of our relationship with God. It is this spiritual connection that provides the foundation for enduring love and commitment. Understanding and embracing this truth has transformed my perspective on marriage and highlighted the importance of nurturing our faith. It is through this divine relationship that we find the strength to overcome challenges, to support one another, and to build a marriage that stands the test of time.

Reflecting on my life

As I journey through life, I have come to a profound realization about the importance of empathy and communication in nurturing genuine relationships. It's easy to become entangled in our own perspectives and frustrations, losing sight of the emotional landscapes of those around us. Yet, the true essence of connection lies in our ability to place ourselves in each other's shoes, to truly understand and feel the depth of another's experience. This empathy fosters a bond that goes beyond mere words, reaching into the core of our shared humanity.

Throughout my life, I've discovered that effective communication is far more than just a means of exchanging information; it is an art of building bridges between hearts. It's about connecting deeply with others, sharing our innermost thoughts and feelings in ways that promote understanding rather than discord. Misunderstandings and conflicts often arise from a lack of genuine connection, but when we approach each conversation with empathy and openness, we create spaces where real dialogue can flourish.

Growing older has brought me a deeper appreciation for the blessings in my life, particularly my family—my beautiful wife and our wonderful children. Their presence is a source of immeasurable joy and fulfillment that no amount of money could ever buy. Money may provide comfort and convenience, but it cannot purchase the love and support that my family offers. These are gifts of the heart, invaluable and irreplaceable, that enrich my life in ways I never could have imagined.

My wife's unwavering love and support have been a cornerstone of my life. Her kindness, patience, and commitment to our marriage have shown me the true meaning of devotion. In moments of struggle and joy alike, her presence has been a steady light, guiding me through the challenges we've faced. The love we share is a testament to the power of mutual respect and understanding, a bond that transcends the material aspects of life.

Our children, with their innocence and unfiltered joy, remind me daily of the purest forms of love. Their laughter, their trust, and their boundless affection fill our home with warmth and happiness. They are a constant reminder of what truly matters, of the values that transcend worldly pursuits. Watching them grow and thrive, I am reminded of the responsibility I have to model a life of love, integrity, and faith.

My gratitude for my family runs deep. They are my sanctuary, my source of strength, and the embodiment of the values I hold dear. Their love has taught me that the most profound treasures in life are not those that can be measured or bought but those that are felt deeply in the heart. Their presence in my life has shown me the true meaning of purpose and fulfillment.

As a Christian, I recognize that my journey is one of continuous growth and learning. It is a path that requires humility, a willingness to evolve, and a commitment to living in alignment with divine principles. Every day presents new opportunities to deepen my understanding of what it means to live a life of love and compassion. I am thankful for the lessons that life has imparted, for the guidance of my faith, and for the profound impact that my family has had on my soul.

Reflecting on my life, I am overwhelmed with gratitude for the blessings I have received. My family is a beacon of light in my life, guiding me through both the triumphs and trials. Their love is a constant reminder of the importance of living with intention and grace. I cherish each moment with them, striving to honor their significance by living a life that reflects the values of empathy, love, and faith.

Ultimately, I believe that embracing these values not only enriches our own lives but also touches the lives of those around us. By living with empathy, kindness, and understanding, we contribute to a world where relationships are strengthened and where the essence of human connection is celebrated. This journey, grounded in love and guided by faith, is the true measure of a life well lived.

How wrong I was!

My approach to relationships and control was severely misguided. I held onto a belief that financial management and social interactions needed to be tightly controlled to maintain stability and security. My actions were driven by insecurity and a desire for dominance, leading me to impose restrictive measures on Sara's social life. This was an attempt to manage our resources, but it had the unintended consequence of isolating her from her support system and causing strain on our marriage.

I perceived any request for financial assistance or social activity as a potential threat to our economic well-being. I was convinced that friends and family members might exploit our finances or influence Sara to make unnecessary purchases. This narrow viewpoint led me to impose stringent rules on her social interactions, restricting her from seeing certain individuals or engaging in activities that I deemed unworthy of our financial resources.

This controlling behavior stemmed from my own fears and

a skewed understanding of financial responsibility. I felt that by limiting Sara's connections, I was protecting our family's financial stability. However, this perspective was fundamentally flawed, as it neglected the importance of trust and mutual respect in our relationship. My actions were not only misguided but also detrimental to Sara's emotional well-being and our marriage's overall health.

Sara's social circle, once a vibrant source of support, began to diminish as I imposed more restrictions. She was forced to navigate her relationships carefully, often avoiding interactions that I would disapprove of. This isolation was a significant burden for her, as it deprived her of the companionship and support that were crucial for her happiness and mental health.

The negative impact of my behavior became increasingly evident as I noticed Sara's growing sense of loneliness. Friends and family, concerned for her well-being, began to question my actions. When they confronted me, my immediate reaction was to sever ties and eliminate communication with those who challenged my control. This only deepened the rift between Sara and her support network, exacerbating her feelings of isolation.

The turning point came when I confronted the consequences of my actions. Witnessing Sara's sadness and the strain on our relationships forced me to reflect on the damage I had caused. I realized that my need for control had severely impacted her life and our marriage. This realization marked the beginning of a crucial transformation in how I approached our relationship and my understanding of partnership.

I began to recognize the value of Sara's connections with her friends and family. I understood that these relationships were vital for her well-being and essential for a balanced marriage.

Letting go of my need for control, I shifted my focus to building trust and fostering a supportive environment. This change involved acknowledging my mistakes and making a conscious effort to improve how I managed our finances and social interactions.

One of the first steps in this transformation was to engage in open and honest conversations with Sara about our financial situation and social life. I admitted my past errors and expressed a commitment to change. I encouraged Sara to reconnect with her friends and family, understanding that these connections were important for her happiness and the health of our marriage.

Additionally, I worked on addressing the insecurities and fears that had driven my controlling behavior. Through self-reflection and counseling, I learned to manage my anxieties and approach our relationship with greater trust and respect. I realized that a healthy marriage requires shared responsibilities and decisions rather than control based on personal insecurities.

As I implemented these changes, I observed a gradual improvement in our relationship. Sara's sense of isolation began to ease as she reconnected with her support network. Our marriage grew stronger as we built a more balanced and respectful partnership. I learned that relinquishing control and embracing trust was crucial for fostering a positive and supportive relationship.

The process of change was challenging and required ongoing effort. However, the benefits were clear. I discovered that a healthy marriage is grounded in mutual respect, trust, and support, not control and manipulation. By allowing Sara to maintain her social connections and addressing my own issues, I contributed to a more positive and supportive environment for our marriage.

In summary, the experience taught me valuable lessons about the importance of trust and respect in a relationship. It highlighted the need to let go of control and adopt a more balanced approach to partnership. Through these changes, I was able to rebuild our marriage on a foundation of mutual support and understanding, creating a stronger and more resilient bond with Sara.

I myself am guilty of this as a husband. Sometimes, we forget how God has blessed us with our wives, and once we get comfortable in a marriage, we stop doing the things that made them fall in love with us—like going out, holding hands, walking in parks, and going to the movies. We make excuses for not doing things with them instead of coming up with better suggestions. We have advice for everyone else when it comes to helping others, even to the extent of giving biblical scriptures, but we do not apply those scriptures to our own lives. Excuses for being mean husbands will not cut it; we have to do better. I would use every excuse you could think of to solidify my reasoning for not doing anything. Once I noticed my wife ready to do things without me, I felt offended. I wondered why I was being cut out of going to events. This forced me to realize that excuses would no longer work. No one wants to be locked up in a house and treated like a slave. We have to realize, as men, that providing is not only financial but also mental, physical, and spiritual. You have to always feed your wife's passion. We're husbands, and we are supposed to set the tone in the house—not be cavemen enforcing demands. What you don't want is for your wife to realize the only connection you had to her was financial because, if that's the case, you can easily be replaced. Do you want your wife to love you when you're at your best and also when you're at your worst? Ask yourself: if you were let go from your job, or if you're running a business and unfortunately you're financially unable to provide the way you used to, do you think your wife would still be there for you? Would she still love you, care for you, and financially help, or would she remember how cruel you were to her and decide to take a chance and leave the marriage? That is something heavy to think about. It's hard to mentally abuse someone when you have nothing to hold over their head anymore. With love as the connection through God, your marriage could stand strong through any weather.

I really hope this book helps you reflect on your responsibility as a man, as a husband, and as a true believer in Jesus Christ. I encourage you to humble your heart and understanding, and to search for the better you by reading the Scriptures of the Bible. The Bible has the potential to help you become the best husband that your wife could ever want in life. The fact that you've made it this far into reading the book shows that you are already on the right path to progress. This means you know that there has to be a change, and that change has to come from God to you. A lot of times, it's hard for one to take criticism or judgment from others. I know for myself it was hard to reason with others trying to explain that I had a problem that needed to be addressed when it came to being controlling in my marriage and allowing the open space for my wife to feel comfortable, loved, and respected as she should have from the beginning. Writing this book forced me to look myself in the mirror and compare my past life to how I live now. When I say it's a massive difference, I mean I feel a whole lot better about myself today. My wife and I worship God together as a family with our children. We both have our own outlets and our own group of friends. We don't partake in every family event due to holidays we don't celebrate, but we participate in the majority of family functions.

I have learned to appreciate the things my wife has done for me. For her to be able to give birth to our children and go through all that pain shows me the strength that men would never be able to have. No matter how much masculinity we may think we have, we lack the ability to endure that kind of pain. I remember watching my sons being born and seeing how much strength it took for her to push them out. I was crying while watching her because she was in so much agony. Women go through a lot for us men, and it's not for us to treat them meanly by bossing them around as if they're our servants.

At this present time

❧

This book should have been finished many years ago. My children were still little when I began writing down everything I experienced in my journal, hoping to become a better man and a better husband for my wife. Back then, life was a whirlwind of responsibilities, dreams, and challenges, but I knew I had to document my journey—not just for myself, but for anyone who might one day find themselves in similar shoes, facing the same pressures and uncertainties.

Now, my children are grown, each married to two beautiful wives, and I am blessed with seven grandchildren. Life has changed in ways I could never have imagined back when I first put pen to paper. I am retired now, with my wife, Sara, beside me. We spend our days walking whenever we can, especially along the boardwalk near the beach. Those walks are more than just exercise; they are moments of reflection, gratitude, and connection. We talk about everything—our past, our children, our dreams—and we simply enjoy the presence of each other, knowing that we've weathered so much together.

Looking back, I'm so glad I listened to the voice inside me that urged me to keep going, even when things were tough. Every day was a struggle, as I've said, but it was a struggle worth enduring. I lived a wonderful life, filled with experiences that shaped me, challenged me, and ultimately made me the man I am today. I often think about my grandparents, about how they managed to stay together through thick and thin, and I realize that I've been fortunate enough to experience a love like theirs—a journey through life that is best lived with someone by your side.

God has truly blessed me and my family. There were times when I felt like giving up, when the pressures of life seemed too heavy to bear. But I persevered, and I'm here to tell you that it's possible to come out on the other side, stronger and wiser for having faced those challenges. That's why it was so important for me to write this book—to share my experiences with those who might lack the wisdom that only time and hardship can impart. I want others to know that no matter how difficult things may seem, there is always hope, and there is always a way forward.

My mother was one of the strongest people I've ever known. She lived long enough to see her great-grandchildren grow, and for that, I am eternally grateful. She passed away five years ago, and not a day goes by that I don't miss her. She was there for me through so many stages of my life, offering guidance, support, and love. Her presence is still felt in everything I do, and I know she would be proud of the life I've built and the man I've become.

There's something I forgot to mention earlier, a promise I made that was very important to me. I promised my wife, Sara, that I would support her dreams of owning a restaurant. When we first got married, I was so focused on my career, on becoming a doctor, that I didn't fully appreciate the sacrifices she was making. She put aside her own ambitions to help me achieve mine, and for that, I will always be grateful. But I also knew that one day, I had to make good on my word and help her fulfill her dreams.

It took time, and it wasn't easy. There were setbacks, compromises, and moments when it seemed like we might never reach that goal. But we didn't give up. After I retired, I finally had the time and resources to fully support Sara in her endeavors. That's when "Sara's Diner" was born—a place where her love for cooking could truly shine. Every night, the diner is filled with the warmth of her culinary creations, and the food sells out before the doors even close. I couldn't be more proud of her.

Watching Sara's success is one of the greatest joys of my life. She worked so hard, and seeing her dreams come true is a reminder that it's never too late to pursue what you're passionate about. Our life together has been a testament to the power of perseverance, love, and faith. We've had our fair share of challenges, but we faced them together, and that's what made all the difference.

As I sit here, reflecting on the journey that brought us to this point, I'm filled with a sense of gratitude. Gratitude for the life we've lived, for the lessons we've learned, and for the love that has sustained us through it all. I hope that as you read these words, you find some comfort, some inspiration, and perhaps even a bit of wisdom to carry with you on your own journey.

This book is not just a collection of memories—it's a testament to the resilience of the human spirit. It's a reminder that life is full of ups and downs, but it's those very experiences that shape us into who we are meant to be. I've lived a full life, and now, in these later years, I'm able to look back with pride, knowing that I did my best, that I kept my promises, and that I loved with all my heart.

So, if you're reading this and you're feeling like the weight of the world is on your shoulders, I want you to know that I've been there. I understand what it's like to feel like everything is falling apart. But I also know that it's in those moments of struggle that we find our true strength. Don't give up. Keep pushing forward, and remember that every day is a new opportunity to live, to love, and to become the person you were always meant to be.

God has blessed me in ways I never imagined, and I'm so thankful for the life I've lived. I'm thankful for my wife, for my children, for my grandchildren, and for the memories we've created together. Life is a journey, and while it's not always easy, it's always worth it.

As I close this chapter of my life, I'm filled with peace, knowing that I've done all I could to live a life of meaning and purpose.

I've experienced the highs and the lows, the joys and the sorrows, and through it all, I've been surrounded by love. My journey isn't over, but I'm content knowing that I've lived it to the fullest.

And as I look out over the ocean during our evening walks, with Sara by my side, I can't help but smile. Life has been good to us, and I'm so proud of everything we've accomplished together. Sara's Diner is more than just a restaurant—it's a symbol of our love, our partnership, and the dreams we've made a reality. And every night, as the diner fills with the laughter and warmth of satisfied customers, I'm reminded that it's never too late to chase your dreams.

In the end, that's what life is all about—loving deeply, living fully, and never giving up on the dreams that make you who you are. So, to anyone who's reading this, I hope you take these words to heart. Keep going, keep dreaming, and keep loving. Because in the end, it's those moments of struggle, those challenges we face, that make the journey worthwhile. And trust me when I say, it's a journey best shared with someone you love.

My name is Dr. Abbott Ford, and I am proud to call South Carolina my home. My roots run deep in this state, where I have built a life filled with both personal and professional fulfillment

Outside of my profession, my life revolves around my family, who are the center of my world. I am married to a wonderful woman who has been my partner in every sense of the word. Together, we have navigated the joys and challenges of life, and she has been a constant source of support and inspiration. We are blessed with children who bring immense joy into our lives. Watching them grow, learn, and become their own individuals is one of my greatest privileges.

While my career in medicine is deeply fulfilling, I have also cultivated a profound love for writing. Writing offers me a creative outlet that balances the demands of my professional life. It allows me to explore different aspects of my thoughts, emotions, and the world around me. Whether it's capturing the nuances of a life well-lived, or diving into the depths of writing has become a way for me to connect with others on a different level by sharing my experiences